A FLAG FOR OUR COUNTRY

by Eve Spencer

Alex Haley, General Editor

Illustrations by Mike Eagle

STECK-VAUGHN COMPANY

A Subsidiary of National Education Corporation

This book is for Waverly

Published by Steck-Vaughn Company.

Text, illustrations, and cover art copyright © 1993 by Dialogue Systems, Inc., 627 Broadway, New York, New York 10012. All rights reserved.

Cover art by Mike Eagle

Printed in the United States of America   1 2 3 4 5 6 7 8 9 R 98 97 96 95 94 93 92

Library of Congress Cataloging-in-Publication Data

Spencer, Eve.
    A Flag for our country/Eve Spencer; illustrator, Mike Eagle.
      p.   cm.—(Stories of America)
    Summary: Relates how a Philadelphia seamstress helped design and make the first flag to represent the United States of America.
    ISBN 0-8114-7211-6. —ISBN 0-8114-8051-8(pbk.)
    1. Ross Betsy, 1752–1836—Juvenile literature. 2. Flags—United States—History—18th century—Juvenile literature. 3. United States—History—Revolution, 1775–1783—Flags—Juvenile literature.
[1. Ross, Betsy, 1752–1836. 2. Flags—United States.] I. Eagle, Michael, ill. II. Title. III. Series.
E302.6.R77S64   1993
929.9'2'0973—dc20   92-14414
                                                                                 CIP
                                                                                 AC

ISBN 0–8114–7211–6 (Hardcover)
ISBN 0–8114–8051–8 (Softcover)

A Note
from Alex Haley, General Editor

Even simple stories have many messages.
A Flag for Our Country is a story about a young
woman's love for her country. It is about living in
troubled times. And it is about how stories
become part of history.

It was a warm spring day. Betsy Ross was sewing by the open window in her shop. The day seemed quiet. But this was not really a quiet time. For the year was 1776, and America was at war. America was fighting to be free from England.

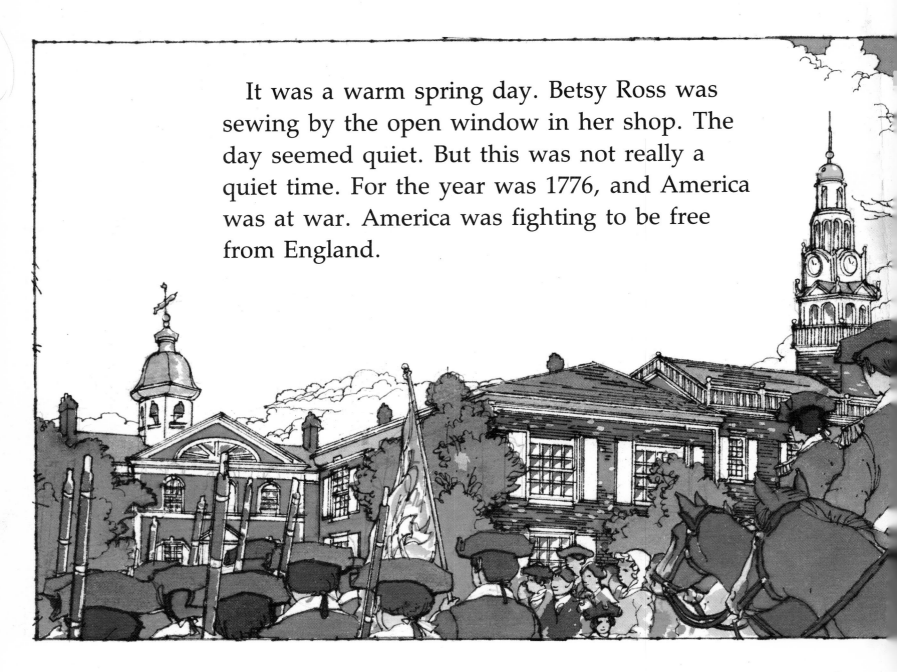

Betsy believed in the war, even though it had hurt her deeply. Six months before, her husband, John Ross, had been killed in the war. How she missed him! Betsy and John had made so many plans. They had even opened their own small shop in Philadelphia for making clothes.

Betsy's father wanted her to close the shop
after John was killed. But Betsy said no. She did
not want to give up the shop. She would run it
alone.

There is a story about what happened to Betsy on that spring day in 1776.

Early that afternoon, the door of Betsy Ross's shop opened. She looked up from her sewing, amazed to see General George Washington in her shop. Behind him were Robert Morris and her uncle, George Ross.

General George Washington was the leader of the American army. He was a great hero. But most people were a little afraid of him.

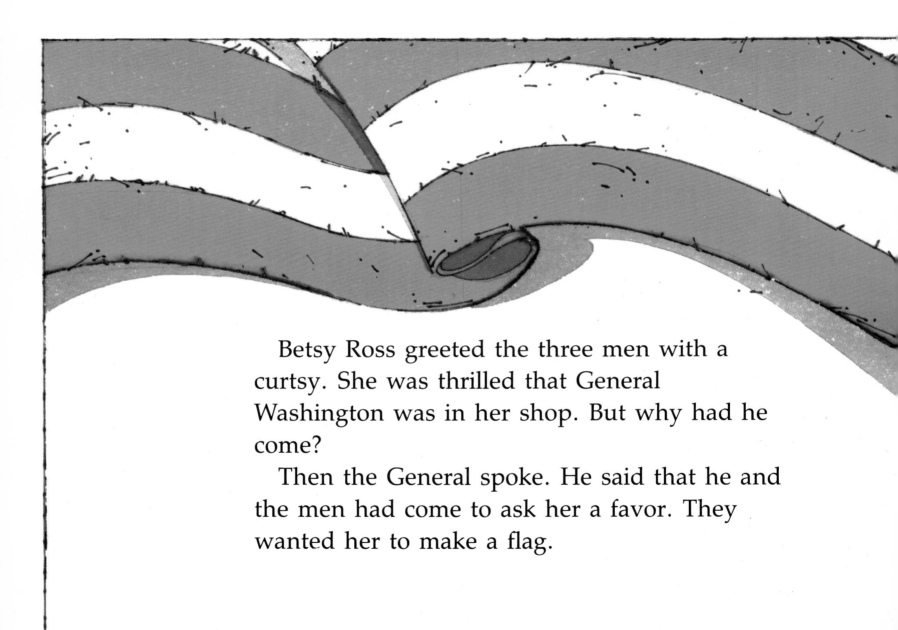

Betsy Ross greeted the three men with a curtsy. She was thrilled that General Washington was in her shop. But why had he come?

Then the General spoke. He said that he and the men had come to ask her a favor. They wanted her to make a flag.

George Washington told Betsy Ross that this would be different from any other flag. This would be the first flag of the new nation, the United States of America.

There had been other American flags before. But now, things were different. America was no longer a part of England, and General Washington wanted a flag that showed America to be free.

Betsy Ross listened to George Washington.
She had no idea how to make a flag. But she
wanted to help win the war. And she wanted to
say yes to General Washington.

"I can try," she told the General.

Betsy Ross led the men to the room in back of the shop. All eyes were on General Washington as he unfolded a drawing of the new flag. The flag had 13 red and white stripes. In the corner of the flag were 13 stars. The stars were in no real order. Each of the stars had six points.

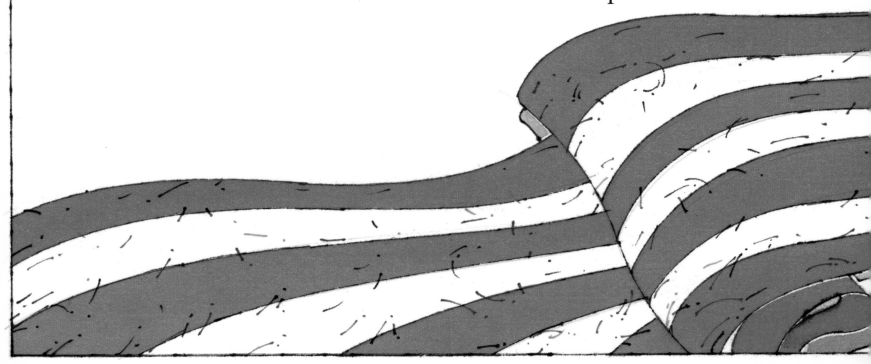

Betsy looked at the drawing. The 13 stars and 13 stripes stood for the 13 American colonies. It would be a good flag, she thought. But it could use a little work.

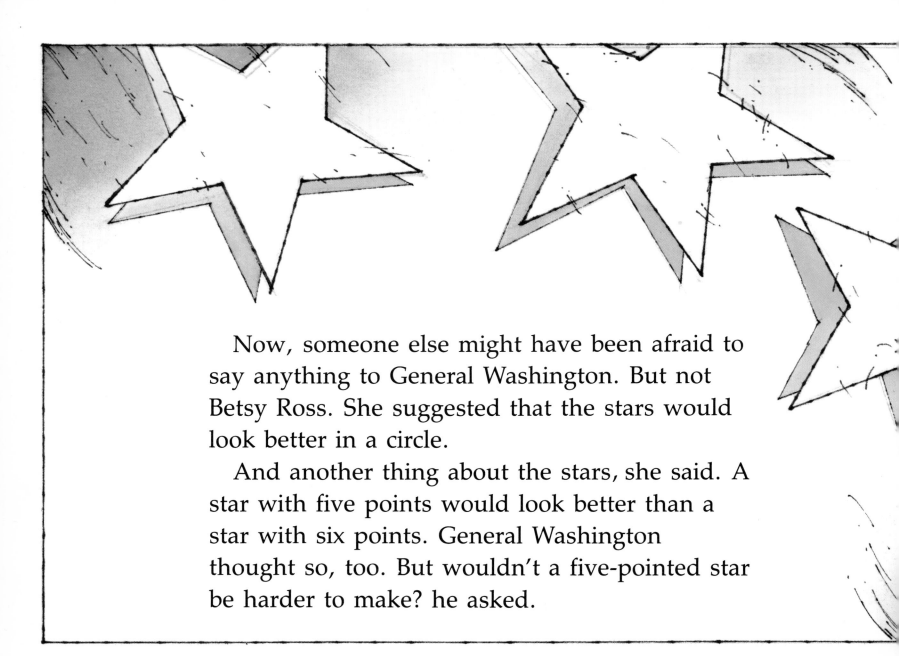

Now, someone else might have been afraid to say anything to General Washington. But not Betsy Ross. She suggested that the stars would look better in a circle.

And another thing about the stars, she said. A star with five points would look better than a star with six points. General Washington thought so, too. But wouldn't a five-pointed star be harder to make? he asked.

"Nothing easier," Betsy said. She folded a sheet of paper a few times. Then she took just ONE SNIP with her scissors and unfolded the paper. Betsy had done an amazing thing. She had cut a perfect five-pointed star!

A smile spread across General Washington's face. Then and there he sat down at the desk and redrew the flag. Now the stars were in a circle. Each star had five points. This was the flag Betsy would make.

Betsy worked hard for a week. She borrowed an old flag to see how it was made. Then she bought some thread and bunting. Bunting is a cloth used for making flags.

First, Betsy cut out 13 five-pointed stars with one snip each . Then, with small, straight stitches, she sewed the stars onto a piece of blue bunting. It was not easy. Betsy sewed and resewed the stars until they were perfect.

The stripes were not as hard to make. But she had to sew them many times to make sure they would stay together.

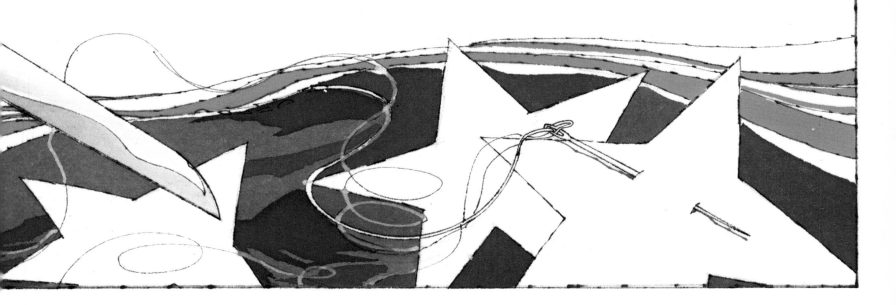

At last, Betsy Ross was pleased with her flag. She hoped that the General would be pleased, too.

And he was. In fact, he liked it so much he wanted her to make more flags.

This was good news. Now she would have work for a long time.

Long after the war had ended, Betsy Ross often told the story of the first flag to her children and grandchildren. And for many years, Betsy's family were the only people who knew the story.

Then, in 1870, Betsy's grandson, William Canby, made a speech about it. He thought what his grandmother had done was important.

Many people believed the story about the first flag. But other people weren't sure. The story was almost one hundred years old when William made his speech. And in telling the story, William could only say what he remembered hearing.

William tried to show that the story was true. He looked for proof. But he could not find any. There was only the family story.

We may never know whether or not Betsy Ross made our first flag. History keeps some secrets forever. But we do know Betsy Ross loved her country. And we know our flag still flies over a free nation.

Flag Day

We celebrate Flag Day on June 14. On this day we honor the ideas that our nation's flag stands for—freedom, liberty, and justice for all.

In 1777 the Continental Congress officially adopted the first flag. One hundred years later, Congress decided to honor the flag by declaring Flag Day.

Over the years, our flag has changed. There are now fifty stars instead of thirteen. Each star stands for a different state. But our flag still stands for the same ideas that it did in 1777.